Richard E. Nichols

Marriage
It's A God Thing

A Practical Guide to an
Intimate & Successful Marriage

Published by Purpose Publishing
1503 Main Street #168 ✺ Grandview, Missouri
www.purposepublishing.com

ISBN: 978-0692480670

Copyright © 2012, Richard E. Nichols

Cover design by: Sharon Dailey
Editing by: Cassandra Tyler

Printed in the United States of America

This book, or parts thereof, may not be reproduced, stored in a retrieval system, or transmitted in any form or by means— electronic, mechanical, photocopy, recording, or any other without the prior permission of the publisher.

Preface

My prayer is that this book would intercede and reconstruct marriages all over the nation by teaching practical principles from God's word that have been forgotten and neglected for too long; with a fresh prospective and humor; and practical guides with penetrating effectiveness. I believe that proper communication, obedience to each other and understanding will release the richness of holy matrimony.

I was reading an article in U.S. News about men and women using different sides of their brain. The male uses the right side and the female both sides. The test of the article was men and women comprehend and perceive differently. The male and female's brain are constructed differently resulting in differences in perceptions, emotional expression, priorities, and behavior. I believe that through the teaching of God's word, these emotional, spiritual, and fleshly gaps can be bridged. Instead of divorce, separation, and annihilation of our marriages, we can have preservation, trust and love built on a solid foundation~ the Word of God. When marriage is down divorce is up. We need a word like practical guides to an intimate and successful marriage. So prepare to change.

ACKNOWLEDGEMENTS

Without the prayers and help of others, it wouldn't have happened. In all things, I give thanks to all who made this project possible:

Apostle Louis S. Greenup, Jr. (The Marriage Doctor)
Author, How to Stop the Other Woman
From Stealing Your Husband!
He brings out the creativity in me.

Dwight Nichols (The Marketing Doctor)
Author, Freedom From Financial Bondage and Gods plan for your finances.

He always inspires me to move forward with my dreams and visions.

Larry Nichols (The Finance Doctor),
called Iron Will by some, the founder and manager of
Nichols Financial Services
Mobile, Alabama
251-316-3606
Asset Specialist

Cassandra Tyler, Secretary,
Destiny Vision Christian Center Church for her many hours of typing and rewriting this book.

DEDICATION

I find great joy to dedicate this book to my beautiful wife, the apple of my eye and the joy of my heart, Ozera and our three children, Nikeland (wife Ebony), Diondra and Richard Jr., five grandchildren: William, Donovan, Nikaiya, (big Poppa) my KJ, and Deonna.

Without my family there would be no book. Thank you for your support. How excellent is your loving kindness. All of you are so precious.

Table of Contents

CHAPTER ONE
SIX BIBLICAL REASONS FOR MARRIAGE........9

CHAPTER TWO
A STRONG MARRIGE IS BUILT ON
OBEDIENCE..23

CHAPTER THREE
COMMUNICATION IN MARRIAGE.....................37

CHAPTER FOUR
RENDERING DUE BENEVOLENCE.....................51

CHAPTER FIVE
WHAT THE BIBLE SAYS A WIFE IS TO
HER HUSBAND......................................67

CHAPTER SIX
INTIMACY AND ROMANCE..........................79

CHAPTER SEVEN
ROMANCE AND FINANCE..........................105

CHAPTER ONE

SIX BIBLICAL REASONS FOR MARRIAGE

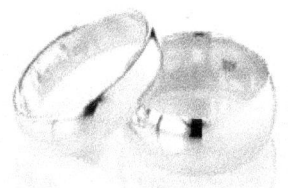

WITH THIS RING
I THEE WED,
WITH MY BODY
I THEE WORSHIP,
AND WITH ALL MY
WORDLY GOODS
I THEE ENDOW.
BOOK OF
COMMON PRAYER

SIX BIBLICAL REASONS FOR MARRIAGE

There are six primary biblical reasons for marriage; 1) **Procreation, 2) Prototype of Christ, 3) Purity, 4) Provision, 5) Partnership, and 6) Pleasure.** When properly incorporated into marriage relationships, these set the tone for a successful and intimate marriage.

Ignorance of these basic reasons can provide an opening for misconception, which can be very detrimental when it operates within a marriage relationship.

PROCREATION

Procreation is of great importance to a marriage relationship because it has always been GOD's purpose to have a Godly seed in the earth. The man who reverently fears and worships the Lord "...his seed shall inherit the earth" (Psalm 25:13).

In this passage of scripture, God, through the Psalmist, states that he would take the seed of a man who fears and worships him and multiply it and possess the earth with it. This is the principle of procreation. God wants the earth replenished and filled with Godly seeds.

And God said, Let us make man in our image after our likeness; and let them [male and female] have dominion over the fish of the sea, and over the fowl of the air, and over the cattle, and over all the earth, and over every creeping thing that creepeth upon the earth.

So God created man in his own image; in the image of God created he him; male and female created he them.

And God blessed them, and God said unto them, Be fruitful, and multiply, and replenish the earth, and subdue it: and have dominion over the fish of the sea, and over the fowl of the air, and over every living thing that moveth upon the earth.
Genesis 1: 26-28

Today, many Christians are caught up in the world's view of family planning. They stunt the growth of a Godly population by excessive **birth control**. This attitude gears to a lack of Godly seed in the earth, therefore causing God's plan to be delayed. On the other hand, the seed of the ungodly is filling the earth. Think about it.

PROTOTYPE OF CHRIST

Ephesians, Chapter Five, shows a perfect parallel between the husband and wife, and Christ and the Church. The husband is the head of the wife, and Christ is the head of the Church.

For the husband is the head of the wife, even as Christ is the head of the church: and he is the savior of the body.
Ephesians 5:23

This passage of scripture gives us a clear picture of Christ's relationship to the Church and the husband's relationship to the wife. The wife is one with the husband, and we are one with the Lord Jesus Christ.

The husband **heading**, **loving**, and **submitting** is the prototype that exemplifies Christ in our marriage relationship and demonstrates the kingdom relationship between the body of Christ and the Lord Jesus Himself.

Husbands, love your wives, even as Christ also loved the church....
Ephesians 5:25

So ought men to love their wives as their own bodies. He that loveth his wife loveth himself.
Ephesians 5:28

Everything about our marriage relationship should paint a clear picture of our relationship with the Lord Jesus Christ. We must ask ourselves is Jesus seen in our marriage covenant? God wants our marriage covenant to be a testimony of Jesus Christ so that others can be won into His kingdom.

For this reason, a man shall leave his father and his mother and shall be joined to his wife and the two shall become one flesh. This mystery is very great, but I speak concerning [the relationship of] Christ and the church.
Ephesians 5:31-32 AMP

PURITY

There are those whom God has given the gift of celibacy. Some have the gift of the eunuch. Those who possess this gift do not struggle with **sexual lust** and are able to walk in purity before the Lord. But those not possessing the gift of the eunuch often wrestle with **sexual temptations.**

God has established a marriage covenant between a man and a woman to fulfill the needs of those who do not have the gift. With marriage we are protected from **impurity, immorality, and fornication.**

> *Now as to the matters of which you wrote me. It is well [and by that I mean advantageous, expedient, profitable, and wholesome] for a man not to touch a woman [to cohabit with her] but to remain unmarried. But because of the temptation to impurity and to avoid immorality, let each [man] have his own wife and let each [woman] have her own husband.*
> *1 Corinthians 7:1-2 AMP*

God did not create our bodies for impurity, immorality, and fornication, but for Himself as a habitation for the Spirit of the Living God.

> *Meats for the belly, and the belly for meats: but God shall destroy both it and them. Now the body is not for fornication, but for the Lord; and the Lord for the body.*
> *1 Corinthians 6:13*

The husband and wife should honor their marriage vows. They should respect each other's **conjugal rights**, showing good will and kindness due to each other. Inconsistency is one of the main reasons for impurity, immorality, and unfaithfulness in a marriage relationship.

> *Honor your marriage and its vows, and be pure; for God will surely punish all those who are immoral or commit adultery.*
> *Hebrews 13:4 LB*

We as Christians should keep ourselves pure and free from immorality. The institution of marriage allows us to be able to satisfy our human desires for intimacy without defiling our bodies and spiritual relationship with God.

PROVISION

God is the key supplier of your needs, but he has made provisions to meet some of your physical and emotional needs through your spouse with the marriage covenant.

And it is he who will supply all you needs, from his riches in glory because of what Christ Jesus has done for us.
Philippians 4:19 LB

God designed the husband and wife to meet the needs of each other. The strengths of the husband make up for the weaknesses of his wife; and the strengths of the wife fill in the gaps of weakness in her husband. God made the man to be masculine and strong, and to be the provider for the family.

But if any man provide not for his own, and specially for those of his own house, he hath denied the faith, and is worse than an infidel.
1 Timothy 5:8

God's word tells the husband to give his wife companionship, to nourish and cherish her. He tells him to feed and care for her spiritually, naturally, and financially; to tend her soul. The husband is equipped by God to satisfy the needs of his wife. This provision illuminates God's commandment to the husband to provide for his wife.

...Yet your desire and cravings will be for your husband and he will rule over you.
Genesis 3:16 AMP

Many needs of a husband and wife are supplied by each other in a marital covenant relationship which God has established.

PARTNERSHIP

The word "partnership" in regards to marriage means to bring equality into that relationship. Even though the man is the head, he is not to dictate and control his wife. In a marriage partnership, the husband as well as the wife must understand that there are limitations to what each can do.

You are joint heirs of the profits of your partnership. A marriage partnership works along the same principles as a business partnership. No one person has the right to operate independently of the other. In a partnership, there should be interdependence upon one another. Everything that occurs in marriage partnership should be communicated and agreed upon by both the husband and the wife.

If you and your spouse find it difficult to reach an agreeable decision concerning a particular matter, the husband should be the one who makes the final decree because, according to Genesis 3:16 AMP the husband will rule over his wife. God has placed the husband as the head.

You husband must be careful of your wife, being thoughtful of their needs and honoring them as the weaker sex. Remember, you and your wife are partners in receiving God's blessings, and if you do not treat her as you should, your prayer will not get ready answers.
1 Peter 3:17 LB

PLEASURE

It is permissible to have pleasure within the confines of marriage. It is God's intention that every human experience pleasure as He ordained it. One of the greatest pleasures of marriage is a healthy, vibrant **sex life**.

The Psalmist said, *"You have let me experience the joys of life and the exquisite pleasure of your own eternal presence"*
Psalm 16:11 LB

A sexually fulfilled marriage can bring exquisite pleasure here on earth when a couple properly yields their relationship to Christ. Notice that this scripture makes a comparison of **pleasure** to the eternal presence with God. Being **eternally present** with the Lord brings joy and pleasure to life.

The Hebrew writer states, "Marriage is honorable, and the bed undefiled." He was saying that it is good to **enjoy** the pleasure of marriage.

Sex within the context of marriage is good in the sight of God. Many people enter into marriage with the so called "old fashioned" mentality. They believe sex is a taboo subject~ it must be wrong to enjoy it.

The subject of sex within a marriage relationship is usually not properly discussed within the Church. So many couples enter into a marriage relationship with the wrong attitude regarding their sexual responsibilities. They feel guilty about having the fullness of pleasure in their relationship, and often do not realize the need for discussion or communication to each other and/or their pastor. Also, some couples never communicate with each other regarding what it takes to satisfy each other's sexual desires. This is most important.

Let the marriage be held in honor [esteemed, worthy, precious, of great price, and especially dear] in all things. And thus, let the marriage bed be undefiled [kept in honor]. You must communicate how you feel inside and your desire to have these needs met.

Christian marriages should be alive and vibrant. Keep the joy in your relationship. Communicate with your spouse. Elaborate to your spouse what you need for satisfaction and sexual fulfillment. God created pleasure in sex for marriage. Your marriage can fulfill every sensual desire you have or ever will have because it is a "God Thing". God is the one who knows how to meet our need for pleasure. He ordained marriage to be the vehicle for that fulfillment.

O Taste and see that the Lord [our God] is good! Blessed [happy] fortunate to be envied is the man who trusts and takes refuge in him.
Psalms 34:8 AMP

The word likens being married to obtaining favor with the Lord. Your marriage should give you the same satisfaction you are enjoying with the Lord. Stated simply, the reason God wants you married is for pleasure~ your pleasure and His. If you are not being satisfied in your marriage, discuss it among yourself. Remember to keep your personal relationship between yourselves.

Let those who favor my righteous cause and have pleasure in my uprightness shout for joy and be glad, and say continually, let the Lord be magnified, who takes pleasure in the prosperity of his servant. Psalm 35:27 AMP

Finding a wife is God's way of prospering you. God will give you favor when you find a wife because it gives Him pleasure to prosper you.

It is my prayer that these six points will become guidelines for your marriage. Let each of them bring the joy of full intimacy and pleasure into its proper place in your marriage. God wants us to know His pleasures, which he ordained for our lives before the world began.

Pray this prayer with me:
Father, in Jesus' name, let pleasure and fun return to my marriage. I thank you for it now in Jesus name. AMEN.

Thank You

Thanks, it is good to say thanks; it makes you feel warm and good inside.
So, just imagine how good it makes the person feel whom you share your thank you with.
Thank you for being you because if it were no you, there would be no reason for me to say
Thank You, to you.
Thank You for how you care, its part of you that let's me know that you are there.
Thank You.
Thank You for being different it's the Balance that matures what we share.
And it makes me very aware of how important it is just to have you there.
Thank You.
Thank You for every good and perfect gift you share. It lets me know that heaven was aware of what I need to make it there.
Thank You.
Thank You, thank you, thank you is what I want to share.
In order to stay on top I need to have you there.
Thank You,
Richard E. Nichols

CHAPTER TWO

A STRONG MARRIAGE IS BUILT ON OBEDIENCE

ALL YOU NEED IN THE WORLD IS LOVE AND LAUGHTER. THAT'S ALL ANYBODY NEEDS. TO HAVE LOVE IN ONE HAND AND LAUGHTER IN THE OTHER....

AUGUST WILSON

A Strong Marriage is built on Obedience

People make all kinds of sacrifices or changes in their lives to better their marriage relationships. Some choose **dieting, cosmetic surgery, or personality adjustments.** Often people spend large sums of money on marriage counselors. Others purchase homes, cars, clothes or other items.

These things are done with the idea that spending will solve their immediate problems. In spite of all those efforts, none work on a consistent basis because they are not the proper solution. In fact, **"short-term"** solutions are often the cause of additional problems. Today, marriages can only be built by using common sense, honest and sincere communication, and strict obedience to God's Word.

In America, one in every two marriages ends in divorce. Unfortunately, this statistic holds true, even among Christians. There are no quick fixes or clear-cut formulas that can be laid out for a successful marriage because all marriages are different. Although society, with the many psychiatrists and counselors, says it has the answer, and though counseling can be of great importance, the results remain the same when biblical guidelines are not followed. While one in every two marriages ends in divorce, one in every three marriages consists of partners where one or both have been previously married.

Our family stability can no longer be depended upon. The deterioration of the family is also devastating to society as a whole.

Come now, let us reason together, saith the Lord: though your sins be as scarlet, they shall be as white as snow; though they be red like crimson, they shall be as wool. If ye be willing and obedient, ye shall eat the good of the land: But if you refuse and rebel, ye shall be devoured with the sword: for the mouth of the Lord hath spoken it.
Isaiah 1: 18-20

Come, let's talk this over! says the Lord; no matter how deep the stain of your sins, I can take it out and make you as clean as freshly fallen snow. Even if you are stained as red as crimson, I can make you white as wool! If you will only let me help you, if you will only obey, then I will make you rich? But if you keep on turning your backs and refusing to listen to me, you will be killed by your enemies. I, the Lord, have spoken.
Isaiah 1: 18-20 LB

Notice that Isaiah said, if we will obey Godly counsel we would "eat the good" of our marriage relationship.

We make war on divorce and separation, and on tired, boring and dead marriage relationships by being obedient to the Word of God and His counsel.

For by wise counsel thou shalt make thy war: and in multitude of counselors there is safety.
Proverbs 24:6

When talking about building a successful marriage, the conversation always signifies a progression. Godly marriages begin with obedience to the Word of God, then obedience to each other conforming daily to the image of

Christ.

If ye continue in my word, then ye are my disciples indeed; And ye shall know the truth, and the truth shall make you free.
John 8:31-3

If the Son therefore shall make you free ye shall be free indeed.
John 8:36

Let us also reexamine Isaiah 1:1-20 through the eyes of another translation relating to marriage. If Isaiah were your marriage counselor today he might give you these words from God~ "Come let us talk over your marriage says the Lord; no matter how deep the stain of failure, despair, guilt, bitterness, shame, mistrust, sexual sins, physical and emotional abuse, which leads to the inability to love each other. I can take it out and replace ecstasy and heaven here on earth into your marriage and make it clean [pure] as freshly fallen snow. Even if you are stained with strife, confusion, lack of communication and separation as red as crimson, I can make it as white as wool if you will only let me help you. God can work it out. If you will only obey, then I will make your wedding vows rich. But if you keep turning your back refusing to listen, you will be destroyed by the enemies of marriage. I, the Lord have spoken it."

This is a wonderful promise! But the promise can only be received if you are obedient to the Word. Marriage is the best thing God could have done for man, apart from sending Jesus for our salvation. It is a precious gift to be cherished.

Let marriage be held in honor [esteemed, worthy,

precious, of great price and especially dear] in all things.
Hebrews 13:4 AMP

Greater ecstasy and joy comes through obedience to the Word. Disobedience destroys God's original intent for marriage. The same scripture also states: "And thus let the marriage bed be undefiled [kept undishonored] for God will judge and punish the unchaste [all guilty of sexual vice] and adulterous." Therefore, marriage can be heaven on earth or hell on earth, depending upon your willingness to be obedient.

A strong, successful marriage is built upon obedience to God's Word and not on sacrifices. This is a spiritual principle. For example, what Saul did was good and it took sacrifice, but he was not obedient to God's commands (1 Samuel 15).

God said to utterly destroy the Amalek men, women, infants, suckling, ox, sheep, camel and ass. Saul wanted to please the people and God, but in order to do so, he compromised. Compromising the Word of God never works. He lost the very thing he compromised to attain. When the troops demanded it, Saul allowed them to keep the best of the sheep, oxen and loot to sacrifice to the Lord. God responded to Saul's obedience through Samuel the prophet.

Has the Lord as much pleasure in your burnt offerings and sacrifices as in your obedience? Obedience is far better than sacrifice. He is much more interested in you obeying Him than in your offerings.
1 Samuel 15: 21-22 LB

God rejected Saul as king over Israel because he was not obedient.

Marriages in America are failing because of man's disobedience to God, as ordained in His Word. People are sacrificing, but, without God, their relationship is at best a compromise. In far too many cases, marriages are destroyed.

Pray this with me now—"Open my eyes to see wonderful things in your word. I am but a pilgrim here on earth. Now I need a map and your commands are my chart and guide. I long for your instructions more than I can tell. Amen."
Psalm 119: 18-20 LB

The Bible is the inspired Word of God. It gives the keys to an unshakable marriage. The Bible teaches that, in the last days, everything that can be shaken is going to be shaken for the purposes of God being manifested in the earth and in the lives of many.

Let us, therefore, receive a kingdom [marriage] that is firm and stable which can not be shaken.
Hebrews 12: 28 AMP

For thus saith the Lord of hosts; Yet once it is a little while and I will shake the heavens, and the earth, and the sea, and the dry land; And I will shake all nations, and the desire of all nations shall come: and I will fill this house (marriage) with glory, saith the Lord of hosts.
Haggai 2: 6-7

It is undeniable: there is a lot of "shaking up" going on within the institution of marriage. God wants the world to know that the only answer to their cry is His Word, which is a lamp and light to a successful marriage. The true path to a wholesome, Godly, successful marriage lies in following God's teaching and living in harmony with one's spouse.

Your marriage foundation can be solid or sinking sand, depending upon how you are building it. Are you building it God's way or the world's way? Is your foundation the wisdom of God or the wisdom of man? God wants every marriage relationship to be as solid as His Word.

Everyone who hears these words of mind, and acts upon them, obeys them, will be like a sensible [prudent, practical, wise] man who built his house [marriage, family] upon a rock. The rain fell and the floods came and the winds blew, winds of dryness, loneliness, separation, divorce, abuse, and beat against the house, yet it did not fall because it had been founded or built upon the rock.
Matthew 7: 24-25 AMP

The immoral system of the world works against a successful marriage. It seems more to favor the **"shacking up"** or **"common law"** marriage. Quick divorces are easy to obtain.

There was a time when being married and faithful to one person was the greatest testimony a person could make. But today, with the destruction of Godly moral values, it is taken lightly or totally brushed aside if one can boast of fidelity. Over the years, these values have been eroded by radio, television, movies, music, magazines and pornographic ideas. Society seems to have brought us to a point where we cannot distinguish between good and bad.

The Scripture admonished us that in the last days good would be spoken of as evil and evil as good. This is all the more reason why it is important to follow God's instructions and heed the wisdom of His Word. This is the only guide we have. It is the only true and reliable path to His righteousness. By using God's word as our guide, our marriage will not be so easily shaken. It will have a surer foundation and can stand more firmly against the attacks of the enemy.

When I learned that obedience was the key to the success of my marriage, and acted upon this knowledge, God began to turn my home around. I searched the Scriptures for practical keys to a successful marriage, and I applied them to my marriage daily, by both confession and action.

Obedience brings the blessings of God, the presence of God, and the Glory of God into your marriage and home. In God's presence is fullness of joy and at his right hand is the pleasure in your marriage forevermore. God's presence must be preeminent in your marriage.

You have let me experience the joy of life and the exquisite pleasure of your own eternal presence.
Psalms 16:11 LB

In the Garden of Eden, Adam and Eve had the perpetual presence of God, and intimacy of their relationship with each other and with God. God's way is not based upon sacrifices you make but on your obedience to His Word.

The way Satan tricked them was by getting them to

desire knowledge of good and evil. This was the only substance God withheld from them.

> *And the Lord God said, Behold, the man is become as one of us, to know good and evil: and now, lest he put forth his hand, and take also of the tree of life, and eat, and live for ever.*
> *Genesis 3:22*

Because of Adam and Eve's disobedience to God, they lost:

1) The perpetual presence of God
2) Their nakedness or openness to each other
3) Their ability to constantly be intimate with each other
4) Faithfulness to each other (Eve ran off with the snake)
5) The ability to enjoy life the way God intended it
6) The woman, her desire for her husband

Ask yourself the question: **Is disobedience to God's Word worth this? Is Satan's way of worldly wisdom worth losing all of what God offers you and your marriage?**

For you believers, even if the enemy of marriage has stolen from you, you can rejoice in the words of Isaiah.

> *Instead of shame and dishonor, you shall have a double portion of prosperity and everlasting joy.*
> *Isaiah 6:7 LB*

Let me personalize this for you. Instead of shame, hurt, pain and frustration of your marriage relationship, past or present, you can have double portions of peace, harmony, joy, love and passion. Instead of dishonor and reproach, divorce, arguing and fighting (where all the neighbors, people on your job and in your church know about your failing marriage), you shall rejoice in a double portion of God's blessings. In the wedding covenant, you can possess double (what you have forfeited) through ignorance, lack of knowledge and disobedience to God's road map for marriage. Because of obedience, everlasting joy shall be yours.

Obedience is the strength of a successful marriage. Obedience to God's Word is like following safety instructions given to passengers in a motor vehicle. Seat belts and air bags can mean life or death to passengers in an automobile accident. In the same way, obedience to God's Word can mean life or death to a marriage covenant relationship. Obedience to God's Word is your haven of rest.

Say this prayer: *"Lord you are my hiding place from every storm of life; you even keep me from getting into trouble! You surround me with songs of victory."*
Psalm 32:7 LB

Let the Lord direct you and instruct you in your marriage. He has promised to do it.

I will instruct thee and teach thee in the way which thou shalt go: I will guide thee with mine eye.
Psalm 32:8

The Lord knows what is best for you and your marriage. He will counsel you and advise you. He will reward you with His wisdom as you diligently seek and obey Him. The blessings and presence of God always follows when you obey His Word. A blessed marriage is a gift from God through Jesus Christ to us.

Goodness, mercy and unfailing love shall follow me all the days of my life, and through the length of days the house of the Lord [and his presence] shall be my dwelling place.
Psalm 23:6 AMP

Here is a practical exercise to build your faith in obedience to God's Word. On 3x5 index cards, write all these Scriptures and confess them every day until they become a part of your life. Confess them or record them and play them back. The Word will not return void or empty. You will see your faith grow on a daily basis. God will work miracles and reward your marriage relationship as only He can do.

Thought for the day

One word frees us all of the weight and pain in life.,
that word is love.
I love you and you are my family.
On this eve of something new
between me and you,
I say thanks for everything.
You are Gods special gift to life.
Fulfill your purpose and destiny for being there.
Remember we live our lives as a tale being told that will
be our legacy in life:
loving God, loving myself and my love for you.

CHAPTER THREE

COMMUNICATION IN MARRIAGE

HEARING IS NATURAL; LISTENING IS LEARNED. LISTENING IS TO COMMUNICATION WHAT BLOOD IS TO THE HEART.

R.E.N

COMMUNICATION IN MARRIAGE

If obedience is the safety of your marriage vehicle, then communication is the force behind a strong and successful marriage covenant. The foundation of every **covenant** is the exchange of **vows** and adherence to the words of the vows. Most marriages are powerless because they lack communication. Marriage is like an engine which needs gas of continual communication along with constant and preventative maintenance.

It takes temperance, patience, and long-suffering to win the race. Paul stated that he **"pressed toward the mark"** or targeted the goals for the prize. If you persist and persevere to reach the goal that Jesus has set for your marriage, you will receive the prize that God has in store for you.

Communication is the key. During our courtship days, we communicated well with each other. We turned on the **charm** of our personality, and displayed our strong, loving and caring character. Later we sometimes forget it takes that same charming personality and loving characteristics to keep our spouse and maintain our marriage.

There are those who, before they came to the Lord, had what we call " **a good rap**." I call them "**Silver Tongue Operators**." If you listen to them long enough, they will convince you what they say is true. When they are born again, they became what I call "**airheads for Jesus**." They have lost their charm, charisma, natural affection, and ability to communicate natural things to their spouse. They have become "airheads" when it comes to communication.

An "**airhead**" may witness to someone on the telephone for hours but cannot last ten minutes when communicating with his or her own spouse. They neglect to romance their spouse or perform the necessary techniques of romantic foreplay, such as setting the scene for romance, communicating in the language of romance, **kissing**, **touching, rubbing**, and **loving** their mate. Airheads are hypocrites.

Tell your spouse why you love him/her, and why you need each other. Talk about all things you admire in each other. Compliment your spouse on his/her appearances and hold each other close. Set the scene for romantic and thrilling sexual experiences for you and your spouse. Let Jesus roll the stone away on the silent movie set, and you and your spouse will become the star actor and actress. Bring back to life the reality of your original love and affection that has become buried in the everyday routine of life.

It takes more than just communicating the Bible to have a strong and successful marriage. It takes the natural and spiritual, ministering to soul and fleshly affections, and the genuine needs of each other.

Here is the principle key in communicating. Strong prevailing conversation always had its beginning in the natural, then ends in the spirit. It is the same with making love. It starts in the natural (flesh) and ends in the spirit. The spiritual strength of your marriage relationship is naturally determined by the communications of your marriage. The natural is always first, then the spirit.

Howbeit that was not first which is spiritual, but that which is natural; and afterward that which is spiritual. 1 Corinthians 15:46

In this passage of Scripture, we see when God started relating to man He chose to communicate first the natural then the spiritual. This is a principle in God's order. When we follow His pattern, we will prosper and be blessed. An example of this can clearly be seen in Genesis with the forming of man.

And the Lord God formed man of the dust of the ground, and breathed into his nostrils the breath of life; and man became a living soul.
Genesis 2:7

Here He first formed man naturally, out of the ground, then secondly came the spiritual. He breathed the breath of life into him. God knows that, if we cannot relate naturally, we cannot apply ourselves spiritually. So we should always communicate first naturally and God will add the spirituality.

Words are the product of thoughts, and thoughts are the product of intelligence. In order to communicate the Bible, one must think on the Word of God. In order to communicate natural, earthly things, you must think on natural, earthly things. What you think is what you become.

For as he thinketh in his heart, so is he.
Proverbs 23:7

In marriage, we must be equally involved in communicating in the things of the world and pleasing our spouse as we are in communicating the Bible and pleasing God.

My wish is to have you free from anxiety and distress. You may feel your spouse is hindering you~ you can't do what you long to do for the Lord. Often this feeling of anxiety should have been considered before entering into the wedding vows (covenant). It pains me to hear people who have been married for only a short time say, " I wish I was still single. All I do is come home bored."

The unmarried man is anxious about the things of the Lord—how he may please the lord; the married man is anxious about worldly matters~ how he may please his wife. He is drawn into diverging directions [his interests are divided and he is distracted from his devotions to God].

The unmarried woman or girl is concerned and anxious about the matters of the Lord, how to be holy, separated and set apart in body and spirit; but the married woman has her cares [centered] in earthly affairs, how she may please her husband.
1 Corinthians 7:32-34 AMP

Give thanks unto the Lord and pay your vows unto Him. When you exchange your wedding vows, you are not just making them to each other but also to God, and now is the time when He requires you to pay.

In all that you do, it is my prayer that you will be free from worry. An unmarried man can spend his time doing the Lord's work and thinking about how to please Him, but a married man cannot do that so well. He has to think about his earthly responsibilities and how to please his wife. **His interests are divided**. It is the same with a woman who marries; she faces the same problems. A woman who is not married is anxious to please the Lord in all that she is and does, but a married woman must consider other things such as housekeeping, her career, and the likes and dislikes of her husband.

The ability to communicate with each other will eliminate the majority of problems that most marriages suffer. Instead of using singular nouns and pronouns, use plural nouns and pronouns. To refer to each other, for example, say "our" instead of "yours", and "we" instead of "you". Practice communicating as one.

As he said, If now I have found grace in thy sight, o Lord, let my Lord, I pray thee, go among us; for it is a stiffnecked people; and pardon our iniquity and our sin, and take us for thine inheritance.
Exodus 34:9

Notice in this verse from Exodus, Moses included himself with the sin of the people. He made himself part of the problem, "our sin and our inequity". When Aaron was building the molten calf for the people, Moses was on the mount in the presence of God. He had not sinned, but because he was a part of the people, he included himself.

If you become a part of someone else's problem, you become a partaker of the strife. If you and your spouse have a problem, you and your spouse must share equally in solving that problem. Practice solving your marital problems as one.

When the enemy brings confusion and puts pressure on your marriage relationship, it is easy to start blaming your spouse or some other party. This is a convenient way to protect your pride, ego and self-righteous position. Always remember it is better to make up than to make war with your words. Always let your words be seasoned with love.

> *A soft answer turneth away wrath: but grievous words stir up anger.*
> *Proverbs 15:1*

> *Pleasant words are as an honeycomb, sweet to the soul, and health to the bones.*
> *Proverbs 16:24*

> *Kind words are like honey~ enjoyable and healthful.*
> *Proverbs 16:24 LB*

> *Your joy will come by the answer of your tongue. Everyone enjoys giving good advice, and how wonderful it is to be able to say the right thin g at the right time.*
> *Proverbs 15:23 LB*

> *A word fitly spoken is like apples of gold in pictures of silver.*
> *Proverbs 25:11*

It is easy to stop communicating when the pressure is on. It is easier to freeze up and say nothing. Failure to communicate with your spouse can cause you to go in separate directions. This leaves a gap between the two of you. It gives place for Satan to enter into your marriage relationship.

While the husband is being entertained by television, or is wrapped up in sports, softball, football, golf or spends countless hours doing yard work, the wife occupies her time with other things. She gets caught up in house work, the children, shopping, Girl Scouts, and the telephone.

By nightfall, when it is time for bed, the devil has already started to set up his stronghold. You each find your side of the bed and no one speaks. There is no communication. This leads to confusion, and from confusion to divorce. Start learning now to be a better communicator. Begin with simple questions and statements~ those that are not so painful.

Work up to the more difficult problems by practicing your new communication skills. Practice daily and soon you will be smiling because your marriage will be safer, smoother, and stronger. Communicating will then be much easier for both partners.

Ammon, Moab, and Mount Seir invaded Israel and they became confused as a result of Judah's praise; they lost all they had because of lack of communication from within the camp.

And when Jehoshaphat and his people came to take away the spoil of them, they found among them in abundance both riches with the dead bodies, and precious jewels, which they stripped off for themselves, more than they could carry away: and they were three days in gathering of the spoil, it was so much.
2 Chronicles 20:25

Fill your marriage with an abundance of love, romance, ecstasy, friendship, excitement and communication. It does not have to be a den of strife and confusion with every evil at work. Drive out the devil and his confusion. You will be on your way to enjoying the fullness and pleasure in your marriage relationship. Your words can build your marriage or destroy it.

> *Death and life are in the power of the tongue: and they that love it shall eat the fruit thereof.*
> *Proverbs 18:21 LB*

If you are indulging in negative words about your marriage with your spouse or someone else, you are going to eat the fruit of those words.

> *Those who love to talk will suffer the consequences. Men have died for saying the wrong thing.*
> *Proverbs 18:21 LB*

Your marriage can be fulfilling or depressing, depending upon your ability to communicate. If the devil can keep you saying the wrong thing or saying the right things but in the wrong manner, he will destroy the sanctity of your marriage covenant.

The marriage covenant is a symbol of the Church. Husbands are like Jesus and the wife is the Church. Jesus is the husband, the Church is His Bride. The Bible is Jesus' communication medium. He's the master communicator and we should pattern our relationship after Him. Jesus always says the right word, in the right manner, at the right season.

> *For this cause shall a man leave his father and mother, and shall be joined unto his wife, and they two shall be one flesh. This is a great mystery: but I speak concerning Christ and the church.*
> *Ephesians 5:31-32*

Let's look at the purpose of communication in the husband and wife relationship. First, it sanctifies the relationship:

> *That he might sanctify and cleanse it with the washing of water by the word.*
> *Ephesians 5:26*

Communication cleanses and eliminates everything that is out of order. The Word of God identifies insecurity and heals it; it is the process of sanctification—setting apart and setting unto; working out the differences; making two become one in thoughts and deeds.

> *Now ye are clean through the word which I have spoken unto you.*
> *John 15:3*

> *Sanctify them through thy truth: thy word is truth.*
> *John 17:17*

Secondly, prepare for future public presentation. Let the world see what change the Word has made in the marriage relationship.

> *That he might present it to himself a glorious church, not having spot, or wrinkle; or any such thing; but that it should be holy and without blemish.*
> *Ephesians 5:27*

In this Scripture, we find it is the communication of our words that drives out **blemishes, spots** and **wrinkles**. Words have power. The same tongue that can say I love and lift one to heaven, can say I hate you and cut one as low as hell itself. It was through words that God make the heaven the earth and all therein.

James says the tongue is **"like a fire"**, it can purify as well as destroy. God's word is forever settled in heaven. Jesus is the Word made flesh. Jesus uses His Word to build the Church. Likewise you must use your words to build your marriage relationship.

Here are some practical guidelines to use to improve your ability to communicate.

1. Early in the morning or sometime during the day, lay in bed with your spouse's head on your chest and talk about the day before.
2. Wash each other with the reading of the Word of God.
3. Make it a habit to touch and lay hands on each other every day.
4. Write love notes and send each other letters in the mail.
5. Become a team and begin doing everything together, pray and play together.
6. Practice all of these things as though your life (and indeed your marriage) depended upon it~ for it does!

Marriage is a God Thing

Always remember life is very short and every moment is very precious.
In this life you do not go around but once.
Enjoy your season for it shall soon
pass with the time.
Flowers fade, the grass withers, the sun comes down on them all; then they are gone.
Do not spend your present looking at your past, but embracing your future for it will soon be your past.
Marriage is a God Thing.

Richard E. Nichols

CHAPTER FOUR

RENDERING DUE BENEVOLENCE

BONE OF MY BONES, AND FLESH OF MY FLESH...
OLD TESTAMENT

GENESIS 2:23

RENDERING DUE BENEVOLENCE

Let the husband render unto the wife due benevolence: And likewise also the wife unto the husband.
1 Corinthians 7:3

The word "render" means to give, transmit, fulfill, deliver, yield, impart, perform, restore and reward.

During counseling sessions, the two major problems or challenges I hear from married couples are lack of communication and lack of sex. Usually, the wife complains because the husband will not talk to her, and the husband complains because the wife will not make love with him. The bedroom is as cold as ice and the bed is divided by a barbed wire fence.

If you are not **"rendering due benevolence"** unto your spouse, your spouse is not fulfilled. You need to be rescued and set free from the attack of the enemy on your mind, emotions and body that will not allow you to release yourself unto the person God has graced your life with.

The conjugal rights of the husband must be considered and the wife's marital duties should be performed willingly in the fear of God. Both husband and wife should be loving, respecting, obeying, communicating and making love! Your bodies are your "due benevolence". Kissing and touching your spouse is your duty. When you don't render due benevolence unto your spouse, you are opening the door to Satan, and you are sinning.

Now about those questions you asked in your last letter—my answer is that if you do not marry,

> *it is good. But usually it is best to be married, each man having his own wife, and each woman having her own husband, because otherwise you might fall back into sin. The man should give his wife all that is her right as a married woman, and the wife should do the same for her husband: for a girl who marries no longer has full rights to her own body, for her husband then has his rights to it, too. And in the same way the husband no longer has full rights to his own body, for it belongs also to his wife. So do not refuse these rights to each other.*
> 1 Corinthians 7:1-5 LB

The only exception to the rule in this context is fasting and prayer. When fasting and praying, it should be discussed before the time of fasting so that the ideas and opinions of your spouse can be expressed. Through communication, you and your spouse can be on one accord and receive greater benefits from this spiritual experience.

> *So do not refuse these rights to each other. The only exception to this rule would be the agreement of both husband and wife to refrain from the rights of marriage for a limited tie so that they can give themselves more completely to prayer. Afterwards, they should come together again so that Satan will not be able to tempt them because of their lack of self control.*
> 1 Corinthians 7: 5 LB

One of the tactics that Satan uses to create problems in a marriage relationship is not allowing full expression between a husband and a wife. There should always be freedom of expression in a manner that should not cause your marriage partner to shut down. Pride in any relationship is a powerful energy that can cause marriage partners not to release their inner self to one another. If this should ever happen in your marriage, do not make your spouse look or feel bad by speaking harmful things to each other. Always make your spouse look like a king or queen in the eyes of their peers. Wife, remember if you make your husband your king before your peers, he will make you his queen for the rest of your life.

This can be seen in the Book of Esther with queen Vashti and King Ahasuerus. She refused to make the king look good before his friends and followers and he rejected her as his queen.

But the queen Vashti refused to come at the king's commandment by his chamberlains: therefore was the king very wroth, and his anger burned in him.
Esther 1:12

That queen Vashti be forever banished from your presence and that you choose another queen more worth than she.
Esther 1:19 LB

Because of failure to render due benevolence in this area of esteem to your spouse, your royal estate is being spent. There are many other forces in operation that will destroy the sanctity of the marriage and bring embarrassment and shame to you in the public eye.

Let us look at two considerations that are due to be rendered in the marriage covenant: making love and domestic association.

MAKING LOVE

Good communication leads to love-making. There are two ways to speak: verbally and through body language. Flirting with your spouse is recommended as a way to set the stage for romancing. It could start with a compliment and a quiet suggestion, or with just a touch.

Some of the born-again people with whom I counsel offer all kinds of reasons for not giving benevolence in the area of love making. Some of the excuses provided are: (1) I'm tired, (2) I had a hard day at work, (3) I've got a headache, (4) its too late or too early, (5) I'm watching television, and (6) the children are not asleep (or the lights are still on).

These excuses amaze me because, before they became born again, they admittedly could not keep their hands and mouth away from each other. When they were fornicating and committing adultery, all they wanted to do was talk and have sex. They had sex in the back seat of cars, in the woods, behind the house, on the sofa, standing up and sitting down; but now that they are sanctified, their marriage bed is dead and buried. Maybe they have never read the scriptures:

Marriage is honourable among all, and the bed undefiled: but whoremongers and adulterers God will judge.
Hebrews 13:4

Honor your marriage and its vows, and be pure; for God will surely punish all those who are immoral or commit adultery.
Hebrews 13:4 LB

Let marriage be held in honor [esteemed worthy, precious of great price, and especially dear in all things, and thus let the marriage bed be undefiled, kept undishonored].
Hebrews 13:4 AMP

So many Christians who are now saved treat the marriage bed like it is an unclean burden. They are afraid to be intimate: no romance, no touching, no kissing, lack of imagination or creativity, and certainly the lights be out! Making love, however, is good. God created it for us; He created us that way.

It is important to remember that you will never find the fullness and pleasure of love-making outside the will of God. You will never enjoy the complete fullness of pleasure and exquisite fulfillment as ordained by God in a sexual relationship with anyone other than your spouse. Committing adultery or fornication is outside the will of God. Those who choose to enjoy the pleasure of sin for a season will have their blessings cut off.

Making love between you and your spouse is the greatest revelation of what you will experience when you go to heaven. It is the **"purest ecstasy"** of heaven here on earth. It is the joy of God's creation for man and woman. Render due benevolence to your spouse. You do not solely own your own body anymore. Since you are married, your body belongs also to your spouse; your bodies now belong to each other.

Some of the hindrances that keep many married couples from having a good sexual relationship are **rape, incest, sodomy** and **whoredom**. When affected by the experience of any of these one often cannot enjoy sex with their spouse. They may feel unclean. It will most often take time, patience, understanding, counseling and forgiveness.

Deliverance from guilt, releasing self and the offender to God, brings one to wholeness. Do not be too timid or embarrassed to seek professional counseling from your pastor or from another Christian counselor. So often, counseling and prayer are the only solution.

Many times, both partners in the marriage will be asked to counsel together with their pastor or others so that both can better understand the consequences of the terrible experience. In this way, both can work through the problems together with great compassion for each other's needs.

I now wish to address a statement to married women. Usually, when things start to go bad in the marriage, one of the first pressures the enemy (Satan) puts on you is to stop making love to your husband. That is one of the worst things you can do. It is like throwing him to the wolves with all kinds of temptations. I believe God makes meeting the needs of another person (woman of man; man of woman) an absolute mandate. Meeting the sexual needs of your spouse is so important that you do not have an option.

> *The wife hath not power of her own body, but the husband: and likewise also the husband hath not power of his body, but the wife. Defraud ye not one the other, except it be with consent for a time, that ye may give yourself to fasting and prayer; and come together again...*
> *1 Corinthians 7:4-5*

Making love is the "**glue**" that God uses to keep

marriage alive and vibrant. When you take love-making out of your marriage relationship, or negate its importance, you open the door for Satan to attack. He will trouble the very area in which you were already having problems, and also other areas of your marriage relationship. So remember: the key to maintaining a good marriage relationship is rendering due benevolence to your spouse in the bedroom.

I also wish to direct a statement to married men. It is important to realize that your wife has a strong need for affection. In Ephesians 5:28-29, God tells the husbands to **"nourish and cherish"** their wives just as they would their own flesh. The wife's need for affection is just as strong as the husband's need for sexual fulfillment.

You must show your wife affection without any expectation of having sex. Do it to show her that you love her. If the husband will nourish and cherish his wife, and let her know that she is the crowning joy of his life, he will not have problems with sexual fulfillment in the bedroom. Sexual fulfillment and genuine affection work together equally for a successful, mutually satisfying sexual relationship in a marriage.

To both married women and men, I direct the following thoughts. Variety is the spice of life. Find new ways and settings for your love-making experiences. Here are just a few suggestions:

Take the kids to grandma and plan an at-home, private party for just you and your spouse. Turn off the telephone and put a **"Do Not Disturb"** sign on the outside door knob. Set the perfect lighting and fill the room with the type of soft, quiet music that you both enjoy. Serve your favorite dinner and re-live the memories of when you first met and fell in love with each other or relate some other very special experience you shared.

Do not be afraid of humor and laughter. Humor is a great antidote to break a bashful barrier or repressed emotions. Remember that communicating in many forms can lead to love-making.

Wives, wear your husband's favorite perfume and the color and type of lounging attire or lingerie that excites him. Have the bed made with freshly laundered, perfumed sheets. Anoint him with a full-body hot scented oil massage. Honor your husband's desires as a God-given and vitally important part of the divine plan of creation. Enjoy your spouse as a precious and wonderful gift that God has given you.

And wives, you can get your husband to do anything you wish him to do if you love him in the right way. I always tell the wives at my church, "You will never get your man's best until you fully conquer him in the bedroom." It is a gratifying experience for a husband to humbly lay in bed with his wife, no longer able to be aroused because she has thoroughly and completely conquered him through much love-making.

So wives, put your husbands on a twenty-one day love making feast. Conquer him and he will do anything for you. Your husband wants a really exciting woman in his bedroom so put it on him hot, heavy, thoroughly and frequently. Exhaust his every desire and total need!

Husbands, learn the needs of your wives and their chemical makeup. Is your wife's desire to make love stronger before or after her menstrual cycle? Be aware of your wife's needs during these special times of the month, and nourish and cherish her toward an exciting and fulfilling sexual relationship. Communicate with her~ listen to her. Pamper your wife with cards and flowers or other gifts~ something special that you know she would like. Let her know how much you appreciate her. Wear her favorite cologne. Put on the underwear or nightwear she likes to see you wear.

Treat your wife to an evening out, or treat her to an evening in. Light scented candles. Give her a sweet-smelling, aromatic rubdown (don't forget her toes) and place little pecks of tender kisses over her body. In these ways, you can also conquer her! At all times, however, be charitable during her special time of month.

It is clear through Scripture that women have conquered their men with sex appeal.

Eve with Adam~ Adam was willing to give up his anointing when Eve began tempting him.

And when the woman saw that the tree was good for food, and that it was pleasant to the eyes, and a tree to be desired to make one wise, she took of the fruit thereof, and did eat, and gave also unto her husband with her; and he did eat.
Genesis 3:6

Delilah with Samson~ Samson sold out his strength because he loved that woman. She kept putting it on him until he could no longer resist.

And she said unto him, How canst thou say, I love thee, when thine heart is not with me? Thou hast mocked me these three times, and hast not told me wherein thy great strength lieth. And it came to

pass, when she pressed him daily with her words, and urged him, so that his soul was vexed unto death; That he told her all his heart...
Judges 16:15-17

Bethsheba with David~ when the time came for kings to go out to war, David was back at home committing adultery with Uriah the Hittite's, wife. The same principle can be seen with Solomon and the strange woman. His weakness was his desire for the opposite sex.

It is clear in Scripture that a man can be saved, sanctified and filled with the Holy Ghost; but if he watches and listens to a woman long enough, she can force him to go with her, even if he puts up a fight.

With her much fair speech she caused him to yield, with the flattering of her lips she forced him.
Proverbs 7:21

You can force him to do what you want if you love him right, even if he does not want to.

So she seduced him with her pretty speech, her coaxing and her wheedling, until he yielded to her. He couldn't resist her flattery.
Proverbs 7:21 LB

Wives, what could be better than having your husbands conquered by a God-fearing, Holy Spirit filled woman? Just make certain that woman is you!

DOMESTIC ASSOCIATION

...Dwell with them according to knowledge, giving honour unto the wife, as unto the weaker vessel...

1 Peter 3:7

...Being thoughtful of their needs and honoring them...

1 Peter 3:7 LB

The word "dwell" infers domestic association. It deals with a husband's and wife's ability to flow together in natural things~ shopping at the malls, going to parks, dining out, working together in the home, walking in the neighborhood, cooking, vacationing and being an intimate part of each other's life.

Just Love That's All

Words fitly spoken are as apples of gold
set in a picture of silver reflecting the sunlight after a
dark, stormy night.
With the window open you begin to dream with a
gaze to the future full of hope so clean.
Through the window light so bright
in a distant in sight
you can see snow cap mountains
begin to melt, from the heat of the sunrise
as it is felt.
It flows into a river of wealth and health
as it melts water falls you can hear your future call.
It's just love that's all.
It's the one thing we can never get enough of
and the one thing we can never give too much of.
It's love

Rendering Due Benevolence

CHAPTER FIVE

WHAT THE BIBLE SAYS A WIFE IS TO HER HUSBAND

A WIFE IS A GOOD THING. YOU SEE. HER FLAVOR GIVES YOUR LIFE FAVOUR.
R.E.N

WHAT THE BIBLE SAYS A WIFE IS TO HER HUSBAND

PLEASURE

A wife is her husband's pleasure, and sanctification with the Lord; his good thing and favour with the Lord. When a husband gets the revelation that his wife is his grace, his unearned pleasure, and the gift of God to his life, his appreciation will sky-rocket.

> *Whoso findeth a wife findeth a good thing, and obtaineth favour of the Lord.*
> *Proverbs 18:22*

> *The man who finds a wife finds a good thing; she is a blessing to him from the Lord.*
> *Proverbs 18:22 LB*

Wife, keep your faith in the Lord. Keep on making yourself a good thing. God is not going to withhold your husband from you, and rest assured that no demons, no devils, no circumstances, and no other woman can keep him from you.

> *For the Lord God is a sun and shield: The Lord will give grace and glory: no good thing will he withhold from them that walk uprightly.*
> *Psalm 84:11*

VIRTUE

A wife is her husband's virtue. Virtue is a force, strength, power, and a goal. You have heard the old cliché, "behind every successful man is a successful woman."

A man is only as strong as his woman. She *is* his strength, his rock! Sometimes, in our strong will, we men forget and become oblivious to this very truth. We go out to witness and minister, leaving our wives at home because we don't see their strength. So we function at fifty percent. Wife, you are his strength in this world. He may not have that revelation yet, but keep praying! It will come if you stay faithful.

> *A virtuous woman is a crown to her husband: but she that maketh ashamed is as rottenness in his bones.*
> *Proverbs 12:4*

> *A worthy wife is her husband's joy and crown; the other kind corrodes his strength and tears down everything he does.*
> *Proverbs 12:4 LB*

> *A capable, intelligent, and virtuous woman— who is he who can find her? She is far more precious than jewels and her value is far above rubies or pearls. The heart of her husband trust in her confidently and relies on and believes in her securely, so that he has no lack of [honest] gain or need of [dishonest] spoil. She comforts, encourages, and does him only good as long as there is life within her.*
> *Proverbs 31:10-12 AMP*

The greatest understanding and insights from God that I have recognized as a husband is that my wife is my

crown, my **dignity**. She adds to my life and makes me complete. When I come short of all expectations of others and they leave me, my wife is still there with me.

I have put into my mind that the car can go, the house can go, the church can go, people can come and go, my children will grow up and go, but I will not neglect loving my wife and ministering to her because my wife will stick with me when everything else is gone. I thank God for that knowledge. And I thank God for giving me such a wonderful and faithful wife.

God spoke to me recently and told me, if I would love my wife, He would love the church; and if I would minister to my wife, He would minister to the church. Now, every time I step out to minister, I stand firmly on this revelation. Thank God for an anointing that can only come through a good wife.

FLESH

A wife is flesh of your flesh and bone of your bone. When a husband is able to see this, it brings respect, builds wife-worth value and greater appreciation. This understanding or illumination causes the husband to care, even as he cares for himself. For no man ever hated his own flesh; but nourisheth and cherisheth it. So men ought to love their wives as they love their own bodies.

That is how husbands should treat their wives, loving them as parts of themselves. For since a man and his wife are now one, a man is really doing himself a favor and loving himself when he loves his wife!

Paul refers to a man loving his wife as a "**mystery and revelation of Christ and the church**". When man cannot love his wife, he cannot love the Church and hence cannot love Christ. Love is the very reason for a man and woman coming together.

> *For this cause shall a man leave his father and mother, and shall be joined unto his wife, and they two shall be one flesh.*
> *Ephesians 5:31*

When you see something as your own, or as a part of you ~ you treat it differently. It is of great value and you do not want anyone abusing it or taking advantage of it, whether it is a person or a thing.

Genesis says a woman came out of a man. You make your woman what you want her to be by the way you treat her. If you treat her as if she is a mess, she becomes a mess. If you esteem her of value, then she becomes of value.

GLORY

The wife is the glory of her husband. The wife reflects in her countenance the spiritual reality of the husband.

> *Iron sharpeneth iron; so a man sharpeneth the countenance of his friend (or wife).*
> *Proverbs 27:17*

If the husband is spending time ministering to his wife in prayer, by fasting, and washing her with the Word, it will show. Her face will shine and her smile will grow. Even her speech and her conversation will reflect the Word that has been ministered to her by her husband. The bible parallels Christ and Church to a husband and wife. We should minister to our wives in the same way that Christ ministers to the Church, and that is with words.

> *That he might sanctify and clean it with washing of water by the word.*
> *Ephesians 5:26*
>
> *...the woman is the glory of the man.*
> *I Corinthians 11:7*

A capable, intelligent, and virtuous woman ~ who is he who can find her? She is far more precious than jewels and her value is above rubies and pearls. The heart of her husband trust in her confidently and relies on and believes in her securely, so that he has no lack of [honest] gain or need of [dishonest] spoil. She comforts, encourages, and does him only good as long as there is life within her. She seeks out wool and flax and works with willing hands [to develop it]. She is like the merchant ships loaded with foodstuffs; she brings her household's food from a far [country]. She rises while it is yet night and gets [spiritual] food for her household and assigns her maids their tasks. She considers a [new] field before she buys or accepts it [expanding prudently and not courting neglect of her present duties by assuming other duties]; with her savings [of time and strength] she plants fruitful vines in her vineyard. She girds herself with strength [spiritual, mental, and physical fitness for her God-given task] and makes her arms strong and firm. She tastes and sees that her gain from work [with and for God] is good; her lamp goes not out, but it burns on continually through the night [of trouble, privation, or sorrow, yarning away fear, doubt, and distrust]. She lays her hands to the spindle, and her hands hold the distaff. She opens her hand to the poor, yes, she reaches out her filled hands to the needy [whether in body, mind, or spirit]. She fears not the snow for her family, for all her household are doubly clothed in scarlet. She makes for herself coverlets, cushings, and rugs of tapestry. Her clothing is of linen, pure and fine, and of purple [such as that of which clothing of the priests and the hallowed cloths of the temple were made]. Her husband is known in the [city's] gates, when he sits among the elders of the land. She makes fine linen garments and leads others to buy them; she delivers to the merchants girdles [or sashes that free up for service]. Strength and dignity are her clothing and her position is strong and secure; she rejoices over the future [the latter day or time to come, knowing that she and her family are in readiness for it]! She opens her mouth in skillful and Godly wisdom, and on her tongue is the law of kindness [giving counsel and instruction]. She looks well to how things go in her household, and the bread of idleness [gossip, discontent, and self-pity] she will not eat. Her children rise up and call her blessed [happy, fortunate, and to be envied]; and her husband boasts of and praises her [saying], many daughters have done virtuously, nobly, and well [with the strength of character that is steadfast in goodness], but you excel them all. Charm and grace are deceptive, and beauty is vain [because it is not lasting], but a woman who reverently and worshipfully fears the Lord, she shall be praised! Give her of the fruit of her hands, and let her own works praise her in the gates [of the city]!

Proverbs 31:10-31 AMP

I Can Love

Remember a heart that loves is always young.
To be great you must love.
It's natural to love them that love you.
It is supernatural to love those that hate you.
To live is to love, as the blood is to the heart.
One cannot survive without the other.
To enjoy greatness in your marriage and receive refreshing from heaven.
You must begin again to practice love until the end.

What The Bible Says A Wife Is To Her Husband

CHAPTER six

INTIMACY AND ROMANCE

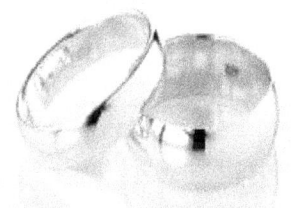

WHAT YOU KNOW CAN MAKE YOUR MARRIAGE GO. WHAT YOU DON'T KNOW CAN DRIVE YOUR INTIMACY AND ROMANCE OUT THE DOOR.
R.E.N.

INTIMACY AND ROMANCE

In this chapter, we will deal with touching, rubbing, kissing, foreplay, and making love~ the things that keep the fire hot in a marriage relationship. Intimacy and romance always involve communication, whether it is sign language, verbal communication or body language. Communication is of the utmost importance. Words, words, words!

Pleasant words are as an honeycomb, sweet to the soul, and health to the bones.
Proverbs 16:24

Kind words are like honey~ enjoyable and healthful.
Proverbs 16:24 LB

In order to have an enjoyable, healthy, intimate relationship with your spouse, there must be communication. There must be words and there must be touching. This is the key, not just in the bedroom, but throughout the whole relationship. Know the right words~ find out what turns on your spouse.

Be aware of the sensitive areas of your spouse's body. Herein we list some helpers.

MALE AND FEMALE EROTIC ZONES

The **sensitive areas** on the body are the eyes,

ears, mouth, neck, back, chest, naval, genital area, hands and soles of the feet.

EYES: you can "turn on" your spouse by looking sensually into the eyes while communicating through the words or touching other parts of the body.

EARS: sexual stimulation occurs through kissing and gently massaging the ear and lobes.

MOUTH: brings arousal through kissing and use of the tongue. Even the Bible says, " the tongue is a fire". It also allows for the exchange of juices from one partner to another.

NECK AND SHOULDERS: very sensitive area, especially when the lips of your partner touches them.

BACK: a massage or rubdown of the back relaxes your spouse. It relieves any tension that would hinder the ultimate sexual fulfillment.

CHEST AND BREASTS: especially the nipples, caressing them with hands or fingers and mouth. The same is true with the naval and genital areas.

FEET: rubbing the soles of the feet, massaging the toes and working your way up the thighs is always exciting and fulfilling.

You should always remember to talk softly with your spouse while making love. The husband should always assure the wife of his love and affection, boost her esteem and express gratitude. The wife should always feed the husband's ego and pride, giving him a sense that he is in control, and let him know that he is satisfying her sexual needs. Each should always immediately thank the other for their love and tenderness after making love. After all, the act of making love is a gracious and kind gift. It is a voluntary gift, through God, to the marriage partner and should not be ignored by one immediately falling asleep afterward.

He is a gracious God; he gave us also the gift of grace with which to thank our spouse~ to communicate orally our gratitude to each other.

FOUR STAGES OF SEXUAL PROCESS

1. AROUSAL STAGE- comes through proper foreplay and romance. Webster's definition of romance is to entertain romantic thoughts or ideas, to try to influence or curry flavor especially with lavishingly personal attention, gifts, or flattery; to carry on a love affair with.

2. PEAK STAGE- when the desire is the strongest, to be released, always a fuller sensation when properly stimulated.

3. ORGASM STAGE- lasts only seconds and intensity varies with proper stimulation.

4. RELEASE STAGE- after the arousal, peak and orgasm comes the release stage where the body goes back to its normal function. This usually takes place over a period of about 30 minutes.

This is what the Bible says about foreplay and romance. Proverbs, chapter six, verses 4-13 and 24-18, talks about what is used to seduce the opposite sex. Even in this context of Scripture, the principle is the same: Beauty, tongue, eyelids, bosom or breasts and chest, feet, attire, and kissing.

To keep thee from the evil woman, from the flattery of the tongue of a strange woman. Lust not after her beauty in thine heart; neither let her take thee with her eyelids. For by means of a whorish woman a man is brought to a piece of bread: and the adulteress will hunt for the precious life.

These verses are simply saying that man can be controlled through his sexual desires and by them be fulfilled. But we want to focus on the things that were done to turn him on or get him sexually excited and stimulated.

Can a man take fire in his bosom, and his clothes not be burned? Can one go upon hot coals, and his feet not be burned?
Proverbs 6:27-28

Can you start kissing, rubbing and hugging the opposite sex and not get aroused? It is like my mother used to tell us, " boy, you play with fire, you are going to get burned!"

And, behold, there met him a woman with the attire of a harlot, and subtil of heart.
Proverbs 7:10

Their counsel will keep you far away from prostitutes with all their flatteries, and unfaithful wives of other men. Do not lust for their beauty. Do not let their coyness seduce you. For a prostitute will bring a man to poverty, and an adulteress may cost him his very life. Can a man hold fire against his chest and not be burned? Can he walk on hot coals and not blister his feet? So it is with the man who commits adultery with another's wife. He shall not go unpunished for this sin. Excuses might even be found for a thief if he steals when he is starving! But even so, he is fined seven times as much as he stole, though it may mean selling everything in his house to pay it back. But the man who commits adultery is an utter fool, for he destroys his own soul. Wounds and constant disgrace are his lot, for the woman's husband will be furious in his jealously, and he will have no mercy on you in his day of vengeance. You will not be able to buy him off, no matter what you offer. Follow my advice, my son; always keep it in mind and stick to it. Obey me and live! Guard my words as your most precious possession. Write them down, and also keep them deep within your heart. Love wisdom like a sweetheart; make her a beloved member of your family. Let her hold you back from affairs with other women~ from listening to their flattery. I was looking out the window of my house one day and saw a simple-minded lad, a young man lacking common sense, walking at twilight down the street to the house of this wayward girl, a prostitute. She approached him, saucy and pert and dressed seductively. She was the brash, coarse type, often seen in the streets and markets, soliciting at every corner for men to

be her lovers. She put her arms around him and kissed him, and with a saucy look she said, "I've decided to forget our quarrel! I was just coming to look for you and here you are! My bed is spread with lovely, colored sheets of finest linen imported from Egypt, perfumed with myrrh, aloes and cinnamon. Come on, let's take our fill of love until morning, for my husband is away on a long trip. He has taken a wallet full of money with him, and won't return for several days." So she seduced him with her pretty speech, her coaxing and her wheedling, until he yielded to her. He could not resist her flattery.
                                    Proverbs 6:24-7:21 LB

These verses also talk about perfume, colored sheets, spices, and dinner in bed.

Behold, you are fair my love! Behold, you are fair! You have dove's eyes behind your veil. Your hair is like a flock of goats, going down from Mount Gilead. Your teeth are like a flock of shorn sheep which have come up from the washing, every one of which bears twins, and none among them. Your lips are like a strand of scarlet, and your mouth is lovely. Your temples behind your veil are like a piece of pomegranate. Your neck is like the tower of David, built for an armory, on which hang a thousand bucklers, all shield a mighty men. Your two breast are like two fawns, twins of a gazelle, which feed among the lilies. Until the day breaks and the shadows flee away, I will go my way to the mountain of myrrh and to the hill of frankincense. You are all fair, my love, and there is no spot in you. Come with me from

Intimacy And Romance

Lebanon, my spouse, with me from Lebanon. Look from the top of Amana, from the tip of Senir and Hermon, from the lions' dens, from the mountains of the leopards. You have ravished my heart, my sister, my spouse; you have ravished my heart with one look of your eyes, with one link of your necklace. How fair is your love, my sister, my spouse! How much better than wine is your love, and the scent of your perfumes than all spices! Your lips, O my spouse, drip as the honeycomb; honey and milk are under your tongue; and the fragrance of your garments is like the fragrance of Lebanon. A garden enclosed is my sister, my spouse, a spring shut up, a fountain sealed. Your plants are an orchard of pomegranates with pleasant fruits, fragrant henna with spikenard, Spikenard and saffron, calamus and cinnamon, with all trees of frankincense, myrrh and aloes, with all the chief spices~ a fountain of gardens, a well of living waters, and streams from Lebanon. Awake, O north wind, and come, O south! Blow upon my garden, that its spices may flow out. Let my beloved come to his garden and eat its pleasant fruits.
Song of Solomon 4

<u>King Solomon:</u> "How beautiful you are, my love, how beautiful! Your eyes are those of doves. Your hair falls across your face like flocks of goats that frisk across the lopes of Gilead. Your teeth are white as sheep's wool, newly shorn and washed; perfectly matched, without one missing. Your lips

are like a thread of scarlet~ and how beautiful your mouth. Your cheeks are matched loveliness behind your locks. Your neck is stately as the tower of David, jeweled with a thousand heroes' shields. Your breasts are like twin fawns of a gazelle, feeding among the lilies. Until the morning dawns and the shadows flee away, I will go to the mountain of myrrh and to the hill of frankincense. You are so beautiful, my love, in every part of you. Come with me from Lebanon, my bride. We will be look down from the summit of the mountain, from the top of Mount Hermon, where the lions have their dens, and panthers prowl. You have ravished my heart my lovely one, my pride; I am overcome by one glance of your eyes, by a single bead of your necklace. How sweet is your love, my darling, my bride. How much better it is then mere wine. The perfume of your love is more fragrant than all the richest spices. Your lips, my dear, are made of honey. Yes, honey and cream are under your tongue, and the scent of the mountains and cedars of Lebanon. My darling bride is lie a private garden, a spring that no one else can have, a fountain of my own. You are likely a lovely orchard bearing precious fruit, with the rarest of perfumes; nard and saffron, calamus and cinnamon, and perfume from every other incense tree, as well as myrrh and aloes, and every other lovely spice. You are a garden fountain, a well of living water, refreshing as the streams from the Lebanon mountains."

<u>The Girl</u>: "Come, north wind, awaken; come, south wind, blow upon my garden and waft its lovely perfume to my beloved. Let him come into

his garden and eat its choicest fruits."
Song of Solomon 4 LB

In these verses we see foreplay of gardens, a well of living waters, and streams from Lebanon. Solomon enjoyed being around her and she refreshed him with her ability to be romantic, and in 4:16, she was aroused and stimulated by his foreplay. In these passages of Scripture, she is intelligently commenting him on his beauty.

The Girl: "My beloved one is tanned and handsome, better than ten thousand others! His head is purest gold, and he has wavy, raven hair. His eyes are like doves beside the water brooks, deep and quiet. His cheeks are like sweetly scented beds of spices. His lips are perfumed lilies, his breath like myrrh. His arms are round bars of gold set with topaz; his body is bright ivory encrusted with jewels. His legs are as pillars of marble set in sockets of fine gold, like cedars of Lebanon; none can rival him. His mouth is altogether sweet, lovable in every way. Such, O women of Jerusalem, is my beloved, my friend."
Song of Solomon 5:10-16 LB

Solomon is commenting her on her beauty.

Oh my love, you are as beautiful as Tirzah, lovely as Jerusalem, awesome as an army with banners! Turn your eyes away from me, for they have overcome me. Your hair is like a flock of goats going down from Gilead. Your teeth are like a flock of sheep which have come up from washing; everyone bears twins, and none is barren among them. Like a piece of pomegranate are your

temples behind your veil. There are sixty queens and eighty concubines, and virgins without number. My dove, my perfect one, is the only one, the only one of her mother, the favorite of the one who bore her. The daughter saw her and called her blessed, the queens and the concubines, and they praised her. Who is she who looks forth as the morning, fair as the moon, clear as the sun, awesome as an army with banners?
Song of Solomon 6:4-10

<u>King Solomon:</u> "O my beloved, you are as beautiful as the lovely land of Tirzah, yes, beautiful as Jerusalem, and how you capture my heart. Look the other way, for your eyes have overcome me! Your hair, as it falls across your face, is like a flock of goats frisking down the slopes of Gilead. Your teeth are white as freshly washed ewes, perfectly matched and not one missing. Your cheeks are matched loveliness behind your hair. I have sixty other wives, all queens, an eighty concubines, and unnumbered virgins available to me; but you, my dove, my perfect one, are the only one among them all, without equal! The women of Jerusalem were delighted when they saw you and even the queens and concubines praise you. Who is this, they ask, arising as the dawn, fair as the moon, pure as the sun, so utterly captivating?"
Song of Solomon 6:4-10 LB

Conquering Intimacy

Six of the most insidious destroyers of marriage intimacy.

1. BUSYNESS

Sandi and Tom's companionship is eroding. Tom enjoys his work and usually works late. Sandi resents the little time Tom spends with her and the kids. Both talented parents carry heavy responsibilities at church.

Even Christian couples live on the run~ taking care of meals, carpools, work, home chores, children, relatives, and church responsibilities.

Pastoral counselor Henry Close says, "It's easy to get caught up in concern over things and events and let them take precedence over less tangibles, such as relationships."

Couples need to achieve balance for their families. Maybe individuals can't do much as they would like at church, but it makes a mockery of church when couples work so hard there that it hurts marriages.

2. LITTLE NEGLECTS

More marriages are besieged by little neglects than by major catastrophes, Rosenau observes. A husband told Rosenau, "Eighteen years of little problems are killing us." Rosenau refers to the "Killer Gnats" of avoidance, forgetfulness, and nit-picking.

When couples show positive caring, they can forgive and forget small hurts. Ongoing neglects, however, bring hurts and disrespect that cause partners to see the other as an adversary rather than an ally.

Close observes, "The time spent on something or someone shows the importance of that thing or that person to us."

Little things do count. Most couples seek professional help when a crisis arises; but therapy can help when partners neglect each other regularly, which is sure to erode a relationship.

3. AFFAIRS

No one could find a more effective means for breaking down marriage commitment than adultery, Rosenau states, since commitment and adultery are opposing processes. Adulterate, he points out, means to water down and destroy exclusiveness. An affair destroys the vital elements of the marriage relationship.

"Most partners are tempted at one time or another to have an affair," Close observes.

"Affairs of the heart can damage a marriage even more than a physical affair~ anything one places before the other, such as work, outside interests, children, parents, or sports."

"A mutual commitment to regard the partner as more important than any other person or thing is the best prevention against an affair."

4. PASSIVE HUSBANDS AND ANGRY WIVES

"Men are not usually socialized well to be intimate companions," Rosenau says. He points out two frequent sexual patterns common to passive husbands: men who are sexually disconnected, and men who insist on meeting their own sexual needs without concern for their wives' fulfillment.

"A woman struggles to make contact with her father and later with males who symbolize her father. Males struggle to achieve independence from their mothers and later with women who symbolize their mothers," Close believes. "Men who felt controlled by their mothers can distance themselves from their wives out of fear. When stress is high, women reach toward men, while men put up walls toward women at such times."

Rosenau names the following things a wife could do to create an atmosphere for change for a passive husband: practice detached assertiveness. The wife needs a place to vent, such as to a therapist, so she won't approach her husband with a gunnysack full of grievances. She could deal with and let go of her hostility and unrealistic expectations. She could then objectively list her nonnegotiables in achieving personal intimacy. When she can approach her husband with less anger and hurt, she can do so nonaggressively and without blaming and ask him for some of her bottom line needs.

It is essential that the husband join the wife in therapy. In that setting, a man sometimes expresses pain and frustration that his wife usually hears for the first time. This broadens the wife's understanding of her mate.

Therapists need to teach husbands a wider range of

relational skills. Toxic patterns in the relationship needs to be identified so the couple can substitute new behaviors.

Couples need patience to change deeply ingrained ways of relating.

5. CODEPENDENT CRAZINESS

Rosenau considers the most hurtful problem in marriage to be codependent mates (individuals who are incomplete persons). "It takes two people to put together meaningful intimacy," he insists.

Severely codependent people have great needs. Codependents bring into marriage unresolved pain from their pasts that they project into the present relationship. When they marry, each partner has almost insatiable needs. Scars from the past, unrealistic expectations, defense mechanisms, hurt, rage, and irrational ways of thinking sabotage their getting what they need from the other.

Partners can use conflict to distance the other. They often move from conflict to conflict without ever resolving issues.

These mates have poor boundaries, so they become enmeshed with each other and allow each other's mood to control them. They try to fix or take care of their partners rather than call on them to be accountable for their own behavior. This leads to enabling undesirable behaviors.

"A solid relationship is built on two whole people who know who they are and who like themselves," Rosenau concludes. The Bible speaks of self-love. Those who do not love themselves cannot love others. Christians often feel selfish when they devote efforts to themselves, yet such efforts are essential to lead individuals to be whole persons who can develop strong marriages. "Husbands ought to love their wives as their own bodies" (Eph. 5:28, NIV) gives support to loving oneself in order to love a spouse.

6. POOR COMMUNICATION

Couples need to speak their needs and eliminate mind reading and expecting partners to be mind readers. Partners need to get feedback rather than make assumptions. A weekly "date" would help partners keep up-to-date with each other about surface things such as schedules and taking care of children's needs. The deeper emotional needs require time so husbands and wives can know what's going on with the other and be able to respond to the other.

"All of us have different communication styles," Close points out. "When another doesn't use our style, we tend to think they are being deliberately mean, or that something is wrong with the other or with both. We need to understand how the other speaks." Couples need to view communication more objectively rather than make judgments about the person or oneself.

Courses in communication skills can benefit marriages and parent-child relationships. Brief therapy can focus on teaching skills and can help couples hear each other if anger or frustration are blocking effective understanding.

VALUE OF PROFESSIONAL HELP

Many individuals lack the skills to conduct a

successful marriage. One study revealed that marriages in trouble never get better without professional help. Couples dealing with any of the intimacy killers need to seek outside help. Ignoring one intimacy killer can lead to others' so troubles mount.

In therapy, family and personal histories can be explored so each person can work through resentments and scars can be healed.

SUMMARY

Rosenau summarizes the following actions that can restore marital intimacy:

Confrontation reveals hurtful attitudes and behaviors.

Repentance brings accountability for one's own attitudes and actions that have been foiled by making changes.

Confession leads to cleansing and restoration.

Expression of feelings brings into the open feelings that have festered and spread poison into the marriage.

Forgiveness turns energy used in resentment into energy used to give caring.

Making amends leads to restitution, which builds trust. Marriage was God's idea. Couples who work at developing intimacy please God. Destroying intimacy killers may take a lot of dedicated, even painful, work. Increased intimacy enriches the lives of the individuals, strengthens the marriage itself, and blesses the children. "Be transformed by the renewing of your mind," (Rom. 12:2a, NIV)

THE BENEFITS OF INTIMACY

Intimacy is touching, being close, talking and making love. According to research, the health benefits of marital sex extend well beyond the bedroom. Turns out, marital sex is good for you in ways you may never have imagined.

1. Stress

"Having marital sex could lower your stress and your blood pressure. People who had intercourse responded better to stress than those who engaged in other sexual behaviors or abstained."

All ways treat your spouse as if you were dating. It keeps the fire hot and relieves stress and causes the brain to release happy chemicals .

2. Pain

It relieves pain. Marital sex is one of the best pain killers ever created. The brain produces these endorphins that act on the body similar to morphine.

3. Don't worry be happy

Marital intimacy can solve a lot of problems. Intimacy in a marriage relationship is like a river of cleaning water that can move you from pass hurts and pains into forgiveness. Remember change always start with you and your relationship with God. It is excellent for relieving tension so you can move from past financial issues.

Intimate moments are worth a million dollars when you are in a storm; try it. The list goes on.

4. Improves bladder control.

5. Lowers risk of breast cancer.

6. According to WebMD, sexual intimacy boosts immunity.

7. Sexual intimacy helps burn 85 calories or more every 30 minutes.

8. Sex two to three times a week cuts your chances in half to those who only have sex once a month.

9. Builds self-esteem. Great intimacy begins with self-esteem. Sex Therapist, Gina Ogden, PhD stated "One of the reasons people say they have sex is to feel good about themselves."

10. May reduce the risk of prostate cancer:

Frequent love-making especially in 20-something men, may lower the risk of getting prostate cancer later in life, some research shows.

For instance, a study published in the *Journal of the American Medical Association*, found that men who had 21 or more love making experiences a month, were less likely to get prostate cancer than those who had four to seven per month.

Of course, that study doesn't prove that making love was the only factor that mattered. Many things affect a person's odds of developing cancer. The researchers did take that into consideration, and the findings still held.

11. *Stronger Pelvic Floor Muscles*– for women, doing pelvic floor muscle exercises called Kegels, it may mean they will enjoy more pleasure and, as a perk, less chance of incontinence later in life.

Websites on Marital benefits:

www.webmd.com/sex-relationships/guide/10-surprising-health-benefits-of-sex

www.marriage.about.com/cs/sex/a/sexfrequency.htm

Practical Guide To An Intimate and Successful Marriage

SEXUAL SURVEY FOR YOUR MARRIAGE

1. When do you want to have sexual intercourse or make love to your spouse?

   Early morning to morning_____   Evening_____

   Noon day_____   All the time_____

2. What is your positional preference?

   Face to Face_____   Standing position____

   Husband on top____   Side position_____

   Wife on top_____   Rear entry_____

   Husband picking up wife_____

3. Who taught you about sex?

   Bible_____   Relative____

   Friend____   Self_____

   Mother____   None_____

   Father_____

4. Do you enjoy your husband or wife when organism is

   Fast_____   Slow_____   In between_____

Intimacy And Romance

5. How often would you like your spouse to have sexual intercourse or make love to you a week.

_____

6. Do you want your spouse to communicate to you while you are in the process of making love?

    Yes_____   No_____

7A. When it comes to making love, who is the main initiator?

    Husband_____   Wife_____

B. Would you like for your spouse to become more aggressive in the initiation process?

    Yes_____   No_____

8. How do you let your spouse know that you are in the mood to make love?

    Touching_____   Talking_____

    Kissing_____   Eye contact_____

Some other way, please list:

_____

9. What is your biggest hindrance to fully enjoying love making?

    Children_____   Telephone ringing_____

Other, list:

_____

_____

10. What do you think is God's purpose of making love to each other?

        Pleasure_____

        Procreation_____

        Relieve Tension_____

        Feel Secure_____

        To stay bonded_____

        Other, list_____

11. Do you and your spouse spend time relating to each others private parts, such as the genital area?

        Yes_____

        No_____

Intimacy And Romance

CHAPTER SEVEN

ROMANCE AND FINANCE

MANAGE YOUR FINANCE, AND YOU WON'T HAVE TO RESCUE YOUR ROMANCE.

R.E.N.

ROMANCE AND FINANCE

If you do not understand how finance and romance work together, you are headed for failure before you ever get started. One of the major causes of divorce is money and misunderstanding associated with it. It does not matter how much you love one another. That love will wear out when the money is an issue.

When going through the dating and engagement period most people are so in love, amnesia seems to set in. They forget to ask questions about finances~ income and credit responsibilities. There is little discussion about savings accounts, checking accounts, houses, land, debts, loans, bankruptcy proceedings and employment history. They soon find after marriage they have inherited each others debts and bad financial habits.

Most of us have been trained by others who failed. They taught us many things:

"Marriage is 50-50 (half yours and half mine~ separating everything)."

"Always keep an ace in the hole (hide a little for hard times just in case things go bad)."

"If you don't look out for yourself, no one else will (always look out for yourself first)."

As a result of this negative training, we develop bad attitudes. We become selfish in our behavior as well. By this, we can see that improper attitudes create wrong directions. When one does not think right, one will not act right. We are all products of our thoughts and life experiences.

> ...Which walketh in a way that was not good, after their own thoughts.
> Isaiah 65:2

> ...They follow their own evil paths and thoughts.
> Isaiah 65:2 LB

> For as he thinketh in his heart, so is he.
> Proverbs 23:7

> ...For our of the abundance of the heart the mouth speaketh.
> Matthew 12:34

We are also products of our teachings and training. Whatever has been taken in is going to come out. Our mind is like a computer, it feeds on what has been put into it. Wrong information or misinformation is as bad as no information. If we are going to win and thrive in our marriage relationships, we need to be re-programmed with the wisdom of God.

> And be not conformed to this world: but he ye transformed by the renewing of your mind, that ye may prove what is good, and acceptable, and perfect, will of God.
> Romans 12:2

> Do not copy the behavior and customs of the world, but be a new and different person with a fresh newness in all you do and think. Then you will learn from your own experience how his ways will really satisfy you. Romans 12:2 LB

You always walk in the manner of your thoughts. We must understand we are no longer two but one. After God made all His creation, except for man, He said it was good. But God noticed in His creation of man that something was not good. It was not good that he was alone. So God determined to fix the problem.

> And the Lord God caused a deep sleep to fall upon Adam, and he slept: and he took one of his ribs, and closed up the flesh instead thereof; And the rib, which the Lord God had taken from man, made he a woman, and brought her unto the man. And Adam said, "This is now bone of my bones, and flesh of my flesh: she shall be called Woman, because she was taken out of man.' Therefore shall a man leave his father and his mother, and shall cleave unto his wife: and they shall be one flesh.
>
> Genesis 2: 21-25

In Genesis, God is teaching a principle to us about marriage and the marriage relationship. When we marry, we are no longer two but one, and every aspect of the marriage covenant is based on the premises of two separate individuals becoming one. It is no longer mine/yours or his/hers, but it is now 100% ours.

In Genesis, God saw that it was not good for man to be alone when everything else had companionship. So He put Adam to sleep and took away a part of him, leaving a void in his life. Then he filled that void by giving Adam a wife, making him a help meet.

And the Lord God said, 'It is not good that the man should be alone; I will make him an help meet for him.'

The wife is the husband's help meet. The word help meet means the woman bands around her husband to protect his anointing. She bands around him with her love to protect him from other women who would try to destroy him and his anointing. The word husband means to band around the home to protect the wife and children.

The whole idea of marriage of man and woman is centered around sexual bonding through intercourse. Sexual intercourse maintains the marriage oneness. Since you are one, when God prospers you, He is prospering you as one unit.

If lack of money can cause divorce, proper management of money can rebuild a marriage.

Be thou diligent to know the state of thy flocks, and look well to thy herds. For riches are not forever...
Proverbs 27:23-24

Riches can disappear fast. And the king's crown doesn't stay in his family forever~ so watch your business interests closely. Know the state of your flocks and your herds.
Proverbs 27: 23-24 LB

From these verses of Scripture, we can see God expects us to keep good records as Joseph in Egypt kept good records. Everything we do is centered around management and record keeping. The Bible is one book of God's records.

Keeping good records is a Godly virtue, and it is vital to keep a good marriage relationship. It also brings peace of mind to the partners in the marriage relationship.

At the end of this chapter you will find a website for forms helpful for the practice of budgeting and money management. If you take time to fill them out, working together, you can set up a workable, manageable budget for your household. Be careful to list all income and all expenses. Look for ways to cut your expenses and use the money saved to pay yourself!

When you are in agreement on a budget, in harmony with each other, you will see your marriage prosper according to God's design. Remember you are one!

Budget Form website:

www.daveramsey.com/tools/budget-forms

www.ingramcontent.com/pod-product-compliance
Lightning Source LLC
Chambersburg PA
CBHW071716040426
42446CB00011B/2092